A REASON TO RUN

A Reason to Run

with Eric Liddell

REID BILLING

Printed in the United States of America
First Printing, 2023
ISBN: 979-8-89109-376-8

DEDICATION

To Janet Reid, the beginning of a long line of faithful followers of Jesus Christ

TABLE OF CONTENTS

PROLOGUE

Paris, France 1924

The heat was oppressive, reaching a record high of 113 degrees Fahrenheit. The seemingly endless number of people packed into Colombes stadium only added to the frantic energy buzzing in the air. The noise was deafening, and the crowd was standing for the Olympic final before the 400-meter race even started. Shimmers of heat waved in the sun as it lifted from the packed cinder track.

The sun beat down relentlessly as six athletes walked onto the track: two Americans, one Canadian, one Swiss, and two from Great Britain. Horatio Fitch, a well-known American runner, was the favorite to win the race. He had set a new world record in his qualifying heat for the 400-meter final.

Gossip circled the track about one of the British runners who was running a race four times longer than his usual distance. Eric Liddell, a track and rugby star from Scotland, was the center of the gossip. He had made headlines a few days earlier by refusing to run in the 100-meter dash, his best event, as it was on a Sunday, the Lord's Day. Now ready to run a race four times his usual distance, he also drew the most outside lane, the sixth. This placed him a little ahead of the starting pack, but quickly became the longest way around the track.

Eric was perfectly calm, shaking hands with each of the other contestants. The crowd began to settle, holding their breath, hoping to watch history made. Eric dug two small holes in the track for his toes as his starting blocks and the words of Joe Binks, a renowned British runner, telling him to "run like mad" sounded in his head.

CHAPTER 1

Present-day America on the East Coast.

Thunder boomed and rain poured down in sheets as Anne Steele stepped through her cousin and best friend's back door. Sliding out of her bright-pink raincoat, she shook out her thick, curly black hair. Patches, her uncle's aged schnauzer, named for his salt-and-pepper coloring, sauntered around the corner, sniffing at her pockets, looking for a treat.

"Hello?" a voice called from the kitchen.

"Hi Auntie M. It's Anne. I'm looking for Levi. Is he here?" Anne quietly slipped Patches a piece of bacon she had saved from her lunch. He quickly gobbled it up and sniffed her pockets, looking for more, tail wagging in thanks.

Levi's mom poked her head around the door and waved. "Come in, dear. He's upstairs in his room. He's very upset that they might cancel big game due to the rain. I'm baking chocolate chip cookies, but maybe you can go upstairs and cheer him up. The weatherman says it might clear up in a little while."

"Oh, that stinks. I'll go see if I can get Mr. Grumpy in a better mood."

"Thank you, sweetheart."

Anne waved hello to Sophie, Levi's little sister who was happily finger painting at the kitchen table. The weatherman spoke on the TV, showing the rain moving down from Canada into all of New England. Anne frowned at the weather forecast and wondered if the rain would ever stop.

Making a quick stop to test the cookie dough while Aunt M's back was turned, Anne stepped carefully around the puddles of water left by Patches and bounded up the stairs. Taking a running start, she slid in her socks down the long hallway, stopping just short of Auntie M's proud display of picture frames showing baby Levi and Anne and a few new ones of baby Sophie on a small chest that sat under the window.

Anne poked her head into her best friend's room to see Levi lying on the floor with his feet propped up on the side of his bed. He was still wearing his baseball uniform, the school colors of black and blue with *Chester Wolf Pack* written across his chest. A well-worn baseball cap spun around on his finger as he stared up at the ceiling.

Sports trophies and school awards decorated every available surface while his walls were covered in posters of the greatest baseball and football players of all time. Over his bed, in the place of honor, hung a world map with brightly colored pins that Anne knew stood for every place a significant scientist was born. Yes, her cousin was a bit of an oddity.

Anne waited for the next thunderclap, switching off the light as the thunder boomed. "Levi," Anne screamed, and jumped out from behind the door. Levi yelped and tried to sit up while twisting himself around to face the door. Anne turned the light back on to see Levi in a tangled heap on the floor, like a pretzel.

"Why am I friends with you?" he groaned, picking himself off the floor and looking around for something to throw. Finding nothing handy, he settled for crossing his arms and looking down his nose at Anne, who was clutching her sides and trying to breathe.

"You can't do anything about that. We're related. But you should have seen your face!" She laughed, trying to catch her breath. "Your mom said you were in a bad mood and for me to come and cheer you up." Pausing to catch her breath, she asked, "So, how did I do?"

Patches appeared at the door to investigate the noise.

"You scaring me half to death isn't what I would have called 'cheering me up.'" Levi raised his hands for air quotes and flopped down on his bed. "I don't know what's wrong with me."

"Auntie M said you were upset about the game being canceled, right? Come here, Patches," Anne said while sinking into the big fluffy beanbag that sat in the corner. Patches ambled over and flopped down on the floor with his head in Anne's lap, offering his ears for scratching purposes.

"Oh!" Anne exclaimed. "I have to tell you this! So you know how we're trying to house-train Spot, right?" Spot was Anne's eight-week-old Dalmatian puppy.

"Yeah." Levi sat on the edge of his bed and picked up his hat.

"Well"—Anne paused to laugh—"this dog is doing really well with asking to go outside during the day. But last night, he didn't wake anyone up to go out. So we thought we had house-trained him. But this morning, when my dad tried to put on his rain boots, he found that Spot had peed in his boots!"

Levi laughed. "How did he manage that?"

Anne laughed. "I don't know, but Dad sure hollered when he found that out because he stuck his foot into the boot without looking!"

Levi smiled. "Do you get the pet peeve of hating wet socks from your dad?"

Anne cringed. "Yeah, that one is all his fault. So now that I've made you laugh, why so glum, chum?"

Levi sighed. Do you know who Charlie is?

"Isn't he that weird kid who's way too loud sometimes and gets really excited over the smallest things? He's in our Sunday school class." Anne's voice was slightly muffled as she wiggled her way as deep as she could into the beanbag chair. Patches had dozed off and his head came off her lap. Waking up and giving Anne a dirty look, he replaced his aged head in her lap, hoping for more scratches.

"Yes, that's him. He's in some of my classes at school, even though he's only ten years old. He wants to be on my baseball team. Coach let him join the team as the water boy because he can't seem to hit or catch a ball. The whole team finds him very annoying and so weird."

"So, what's the problem?"

"Charlie wants to be friends with me. He wants to come to all the after-game parties, and no one wants to invite him." Levi found his baseball and started throwing it up in the air and catching it.

"I still don't understand what the problem is. I think you should at least try to be friends with him. Who cares what the rest of the team thinks?"

Levi threw a pillow at her and said, "I care what my teammates think. What if they think I'm just as strange as Charlie is? What if they try to get me off the team? Or even worse"—Levi waved his arms—"they don't want to be friends with me anymore?"

Anne calmly tucked the pillow behind her head. "You are such a drama queen. First of all, you're one of their best players. Second, it's silly to think they'll kick you off the team just for being nice."

Levi flopped back down on the bed, watching the rain run down his window. "I don't know what to do. But I want this rain to stop! It's washing out the field."

A lightning bolt split the sky just as a roar of thunder shook the house. The lights flickered, then turned off.

"Aw shoot," Levi said. "Hold on, let me see if there's a flashlight somewhere." The bed squeaked and the sound of his bedside drawer opening filled the silence.

Anne held her breath, waiting for him to find his flashlight.

An eerie voice floated from the dark hallway. "Looking for this?"

CHAPTER 2

Anne screamed, and Levi jumped up off his bed to face the door. A face floated from the dark hallway, illuminated by a flashlight smiling like a creepy clown.

"Mom!" Levi yelled as his mom turned the light up to brighten the room, showing Anne with the pillow clamped over her head, her dark eyes wide open. "Why is everyone scaring me today? I don't appreciate people taking advantage of me like that."

"Then don't make yourself such an easy target." Anne laughed, taking the flashlight. "It's not our fault that you can't handle jump scares. You can't even watch *Jurassic Park* in the daytime."

"I'm sorry, sweetheart." Levi's mom reached out and ran her fingers through his dirty blonde hair, trying to smooth his ruffled feathers. "Since the power went out, the oven and the mixer turned off so the cookies are on hold and possibly ruined if the power doesn't come back on soon."

Thunder boomed again, and this time Anne collapsed onto Levi's bed with dramatic flair. "What are we going to do now?"

"Why don't you guys go upstairs to the attic and look through the old clubhouse you used to play in? You haven't been up there in a while. Since Grandma moved out of her house, we have some of her stuff up there. There's a couch and some other stuff that you can move around."

"Let's go, that sounds more fun than sitting around here watching the rain fall." Levi grabbed the flashlight and left his room, following his mom down the hall till she went down the stairs. Levi pointed the flashlight at the wall, looking for the knob that showed where the hidden door to the attic was. Anne saw it first, grabbed it, and pulled. The door popped open, revealing a staircase into darkness.

Anne grabbed the backup flashlight on the bottom step, left there for just such occasions, and led the charge up the stairs, disappearing into the darkness. "Heads up!" Levi ducked, just missing a low-hanging beam that was very inconveniently placed directly at the top of the stairs. The flashlights shone their light over the mountains of old furniture and boxes held together with duct tape, looking like a deserted and dusty mountain range inside the attic. The rain was much louder, hammering the roof over their heads.

A strange feeling pricked at the back of Levi's neck as if there was something important to find. "Wow, I didn't know we got this much of Grandma's stuff."

Anne's voice echoed from under a table, "Most of this stuff is junk or really old. What are we supposed to do with it? Oh look! I found a key." Her head popped up with a cobweb stuck in her curls. She handed him a heavy metal key that fit in his hand. "What does it go to?"

"I don't know." Levi looked at the key in the light of the flashlight. Its rough and handmade look intrigued him. "Let's look around and see if we can find something that's locked."

Anne ducked back under the pile and Levi heard her bumping around and watched as she cast strange shadows on the roof and walls with her flashlight. Levi worked his way around the outside of the pile, peeking into boxes and making sure he didn't hit his head on the low-hanging eaves. Under the window, lit up by another blot of lighting, sat an old worn chest. Just like treasure chests in pirate movies, the wood chest had deep scratches and marks on it.

"Hey Annie, I think I found it," Levi said, eyes wide at the sight of the chest. He looked at the key in his hand.

A large crash sounded from Anne's general direction. In a very dramatic tone, she proclaimed, "I've been impaled by an umbrella!" She appeared next to Levi with the offending umbrella in one hand and wearing a bright-purple hat with fake birds and flowers on it on her head.

"I don't like it when you call me Annie, I'm not a redheaded orphan." Anne struck a pose. "Look at this hat. Isn't it fun? I found it in a box labeled 'hats' and I wanted to know what was in the box. Isn't it fabulous?"

"You confuse me sometimes."

"Give me the key! You're taking too long." Anne snatched the key from his hand and knelt. "Being the school's all-star athlete and champion trivia leader, you're not very curious." She slid the key into the lock and turned it. The click of the lock was loud despite the rain drumming on the roof.

Levi leaned forward and helped lift the chest's heavy lid. Inside, instead of lost treasure, there sat piles of books and old papers. A few stray dust bunnies twirled in the air in the glow of the flashlights.

"No treasure? This stinks. I thought it would be something good." Anne sat down and crossed her arms, the hat slipping down over her ear.

"What did you expect? Gold and jewels?" Levi had his head deep in the chest, digging through the books and papers. "This is Grandma's chest. We're lucky it's not full of clothes or something." He pulled out several books and set them in a stack on the floor.

"Well, clothes would have been more fun because I could have cut them up and made new patches to add to my collection." Anne leaned forward to look again to see if she missed something interesting. Finding an old tin button box, she opened it. "I don't like reading as much as you do."

Levi sat down and started looking through the pile of books on the floor. He stopped on the second-to-last book. *The Flying Scotsman, Olympic Champion* marched across the top of the cover in bold, newspaper-headline type. Below that, a black-and-white picture of a man sprinting toward the finish line in front of a large crowd with his face lifted toward the sky. In the light of the flashlight, the book's sides looked like they were glowing. "Anne… look at this."

"What?"

"The book is glowing."

"No way. You're just trying to get me away from the coin collection I just found," scoffed Anne.

"I'm being serious. Look! The man in the picture is running across the cover."

Anne dropped the button box and scooted over to look at the book in Levi's hands. Sure enough, the pages had started to glow and the little man on the cover was running across the cover. The little man ran faster and faster till he reached the edge of the book and it flew open.

Light exploded out of the open book pages and the little man kept running over the pages, making them turn faster and faster. The wind whipped up from under his heels and swirled around the attic, rattling the room. Levi dropped the book on the floor and backed away. The book spread out, growing larger and larger. The words on the page swirled till they were an indistinguishable blur of changing colors. Anne grabbed onto his sleeve as the wind seemed to drag them closer to the book.

"What do we do?" Anne yelled into Levi's ear.

"I'm going to try and close it!" Levi yelled back, leaning down toward the book still open on the floor. "Hold on to my shirt so I don't fall in."

Anne grabbed two handfuls of his jersey as he bent toward the book. Without warning, the book dropped through the floor, leaving Levi and Anne balancing on the edge of a chasm. Colors danced and blended down the sides of the chasm, the wind still rattling the attic. The book lay way down at the bottom, pages still turning.

Suddenly, a strong gust of wind pushed Anne forward, crashing into Levi and sending both down into the glowing chasm.

"WOAH!"

CHAPTER 3

Silence. The wind had stopped but it was suddenly very cold. Anne opened her eyes and gasped, grabbing at Levi's arm.

Levi's eyes snapped open, and he looked around. "Where are we?"

They were perched on the back of an open flatbed truck, surrounded by packages wrapped in brown paper with a bold *Red Cross* stamped on all sides. A deserted countryside, dotted with small huts and wide-open fields, lay before them. The gray sky attempted to keep the sun covered with thinning clouds and fog.

The truck lurched and groaned, creeping toward a high wall and rusted iron gates that slowly swept open to let the truck roll in. The gates were pushed shut by unseen people outside. The truck slowed to a stop in an open section of ground that was surrounded by a tall stone wall with barbed wire strung across the top of the wall. At regular intervals, wooden structures grew from the wall with spotlights mounted on them and long gun barrels stuck through the slats.

The few people who had been walking through the courtyard saw the truck and started running and shouting at the driver.

"Quick, let's get down before something happens," Levi said, pointing to the crowd coming at them. Levi and Anne jumped off the truck quickly to avoid the growing crush of people surging toward them. Backing up against a building to avoid the growing crowd, Levi looked around. Low, long buildings stretched near the walls and two taller buildings stood at the far end of the compound. The words "HOSPITAL" and "DINING HALL" were painted on the front of the buildings.

"What am I wearing?" Anne looked down in disgust at a dark-brown dress and heavy black shoes. She pointed at Levi and laughed. "You look like an old-time paper boy."

Levi looked down at his dark blue pants and gray jacket. He reached up and pulled off an old-fashioned newsie cap. "What's going on? I think we might be in a prison camp," Levi said, searching through his pockets.

"I didn't steal that much cookie dough, I promise," Anne said with wide eyes and a guilty look.

"Don't be ridiculous. We must be here for a reason. Look at this." Levi pulled a newspaper clipping out of his pocket and read it aloud. "'March 12, 1943, all foreigners to the country of China are to report to Weihsien Internment Camp for holding. No foreigners are allowed to leave China to return to their home countries.' Well, that explains the barbed wire," Levi said, tucking the paper back into his pocket.

The wind picked up suddenly, bringing the smell of a porta-potty left too long in the summer sun at the county fair. "Ew!" Anne grabbed the collar of her dress to cover her nose. "What are we supposed to do?"

Just then, a young boy with blonde hair and blue eyes came sprinting around the corner of the building. Behind him came a soldier carrying a long rifle across his back. The soldier was dressed in an olive-green jacket and pants with red rectangles with a gold star embroidered on his collar. He had on a hat that shielded his face with a scowl seemingly permanently etched in. He started yelling at the three children in a language neither Levi nor Anne could understand.

The boy slid to a stop in front of Levi and Anne and looked at them. "Hello there. Did you just come in on the truck?" the boy asked in a British accent, pointing to the truck that was now being unloaded in an orderly fashion.

Levi and Anne looked at each other and didn't know what to say. The boy took off running and passed them. "Hurry, come with me. We're supposed to be in school. I'll explain everything there."

Rather than staying put and being yelled at by the guard, Levi and Anne hurried after the boy. "Who are you?" Anne panted.

"Where are we going?" Levi looked down at his shoes, which were much heavier than his normal running shoes.

"My name is Peter. Hurry, all children are supposed to be in school right now. They'll make us do extra work duties if we dawdle too much longer. This way for a shortcut!"

Peter led Levi and Anne through a narrow opening where two buildings came slightly too close together. The guard slid to a stop and glared through the gap before turning away.

They ran toward a run-down stable in the corner of the compound. Peter pushed open the door and entered a makeshift schoolroom. A barrel sat in the front of the room that was dimly lit, coughing out smoke like an old man with a pipe. The weak sun leaked through the paper-covered windows, lighting up rows of children of all different ages sitting on rows of backless benches. At the sound of the door opening and the whistle of cold air, everyone turned to look. A crash sounded from the corner as one of the students turned too quickly and caused the bench to twist and collapse, sending all three of them to the floor.

"Uncle Eric," said Peter, struggling to close the door against the cold wind and the smell. "Look what I found—they came in on the Red Cross truck. They were standing by the men's dormitories. I forgot my pencil in my room. One of the soldiers was yelling at me because I wasn't here on time. I brought them here as quickly as I could."

At the mention of the Red Cross truck, the other children began talking excitedly and rushed to the windows to peek out through the rips in the paper.

"Thank you, Peter. Good work. Calm down, everyone. Let the Red Cross committee organize the boxes and we will have our share soon enough." A taller, thin, white man stood at the front of the room. What little hair was left on his head was blonde, but his eyes were a clear blue that sparkled with kindness. A makeshift blackboard, which was a square outline in coal dust on the wood of the back wall, had the day's lesson written out. The wind whistled through the cracks in the walls and under the door, stirring up coal dust from the stove and causing the whole room to start coughing.

"Come, stand by the fire and try to warm up. Everyone in the back row, it's your turn to come up to the front by the fire." The man called Uncle Eric spoke with a soft

Scottish accent, motioning them to the front of the room. "My name is Eric Liddell, but everyone calls me Uncle Eric, which you can do as well. What are your names and where are you from?"

"I'm Levi and this is Anne. We're from America. Where are we, exactly?" Levi asked, reaching out his hands over the fire.

Uncle Eric reached down and reset the board on the two overturned buckets that made up the bench and motioned for Anne and Levi to sit down. Anne sat down carefully, not wanting to end up on the coal-dust-covered floor. As she set her feet down, a young girl stopped her and said, "Please don't put your feet right there. Uncle Eric hasn't checked my math problem yet."

Anne looked down to see a math equation written out in the coal dust on the floor.

Uncle Eric looked down, and after a few moments smiled and said, "Well done, Emily. You understand the concept correctly." Turning to the rest of the room, he asked, "Is everyone finished with the last problem?"

A resounding "Yes!" came from the rest of the students.

"Well done. In light of the Red Cross packages coming, our new arrivals, and that it's almost lunchtime, let's end for the morning and clean up." He turned to Levi and Anne. "Over lunch, I'll explain where you are and why you're here."

Bustle immediately started up as soon as Uncle Eric stopped speaking. Peter asked Levi to help him break down and stack the benches against the wall. Anne helped sweep the evidence of math from the floor. The coal dust was carefully picked up and placed in a bucket for tomorrow's lessons. The girl whose name was Elenore explained that when the fire could no longer burn, the coal dust was reused to make more fuel or used for writing and inks.

Uncle Eric stood by the door, overseeing the cleanup. Once everything had been put away, he said, "Alright lairds and ladies, it's time for dinner."

CHAPTER 4

The group of children struggled into their thin, threadbare coats to brave the icy wind; some only wore sweaters, having handed their coats to those who didn't have any. Uncle Eric positioned himself at the head of the line for the brief walk across the courtyard to the building with "DINING HALL" written over the door. Levi and Anne joined the group and looked around wide-eyed at all the people streaming into the building. Hundreds of people from all different places, including a large group of monks and nuns.

Inside the door, a small stack of chipped, mismatched bowls and all manner of spoons sat ready for use. Peter motioned to Levi. "Get a bowl and spoon. Most of us bring our own if we remember." He fished out a bowl and spoon from his bag that was slung around his arm. Levi took a bowl and a spoon for himself and handed Anne a set as well.

"Mine has a little bird painted on the bottom," Anne said, pleased with Levi's choice.

As they gathered in lines to get lunch, Uncle Eric pointed out a few interesting people. Bankers from England, American and Australian missionaries, workers from South Africa and monks from Northern China. No one pushed or shoved. The crowds just waited in line for their turn in front of the large cauldrons that were sending up steam.

They held out their bowls to a lady wearing a big apron, who carefully ladled a thin soup with mystery chunks bobbing around into their bowls. As they shuffled farther down the line, a thick chunk of bread was handed to each. Anne and Levi joined the song of thank yous from the other children and followed them to sit at long tables that filled the rest of the room.

Uncle Eric sat across from Levi and Anne and, over the top of his soup bowl, asked, "How long have you been in China?"

Levi and Anne looked at each other and Levi said, "We were just taken straight here from America. We're a little confused by why all these people are here as well?"

Anne looked at Levi with raised eyebrows.

Uncle Eric didn't notice the look between Anne and Levi. "This is the Courtyard of the Happy Way, also known as Weihsien Internment Camp. It used to be a Christian mission outpost before the Japanese took over. Before the war started, the Japanese had started slowly taking over China. After the attack on Pearl Harbor, the Japanese fully moved in and took control."

He paused, dipping his bread in the broth. "For a while we were safe, and the Japanese only patrolled the streets and made minor changes. But as the war got worse, they forced all the Westerners in the northern area of China to move into this camp for holding. By the grace of God, I sent my wife, who was pregnant with my third daughter and two older daughters, back to Canada before I was forced to move here. I couldn't stand to see my family suffer as we do."

"You have children?" Anne asked, trying very hard not to spit out the unpleasant-tasting food. "What are their names?"

"Florence is my wife. I call her Flo. She's a nurse. Patricia is my eldest—she's five, almost six now. Then there's Heather, named for the flowers that grow near my old home in Scotland. She's four. My littlest lassie is Maureen, she's nearly two and a half. I've never met her. Flo was expecting her when I sent them back to Canada to live with her parents." Uncle Eric paused, his eyes growing distant and misty.

A loud clanging from the kitchen startled him back into the present. Anne's own eyes shone with tears. "Don't cry for me, dear lass." Uncle Eric smiled warmly at her. "Those who believe in the Lord never truly say goodbye. Now"—he clapped his hands together—"dinner is over, let's get on with the chores. Anne, would you please stay in here and help with the dishes and the cleanup? Levi, if you would join Peter and some of the other boys to help bring water here and for the dormitories, it would be a big help."

Anne pulled a face but didn't say anything, joining the line of girls and little boys who were also assigned dish chores. At least she got to stay inside near the hot kitchen fires. Levi pulled on his coat and followed Peter out the door into the cold wind.

Levi looked over at Peter and asked, "Why are you here?"

Peter pulled his cap lower on his head. "My parents are missionaries in a different part of China. I was at the Tientsin Anglo-Chinese College where Uncle Eric taught. It's an all-boys school. Since I'm a foreigner in China, I was brought here with Uncle Eric. The Japanese closed the school, anyway."

"Are your parents here with you?" Levi asked, getting in line near the well and grabbing a bucket.

"No, they were brought back to England by our mission organization last year before the Japanese invasion. They decided to let me stay at school here. I didn't want to go back to England, I like it here better. My grandma likes to make me wear suits and sit on an itchy couch for hours. Once the Japanese invaded, my parents tried to send for me to bring me back to England. But by then it was too late." Peter took his turn at the pump and showed Levi how to fill two buckets simultaneously.

Levi took a bucket in each hand and followed Peter back to the dining hall, but went around the back. He noticed Uncle Eric leaving the kitchen wearing a piece of flowered cloth over his nose and mouth, carrying a bucket, and walking with some of the monks. "Where is he going?"

Peter pushed open the back door to the kitchen. "The monks are the only ones willing to clean the bathrooms, there are only twenty loos for almost two thousand people. Uncle Eric helps them clean if he isn't helping with a different work detail. He's probably the most willing and helpful person in camp. Uncle Eric is my favorite teacher. He ran the sports program at the school. A lot of the Chinese boys didn't like sports. You would think that they would be honored to learn from one of the best runners of our time, and an Olympic gold medalist to boot."

"Wait, what? Uncle Eric is a gold medalist?" Levi asked, stunned. "What's he doing in China?"

Peter didn't hear Levi's question over the clamor of the dishes being washed and people talking as they scrubbed down the tables and floors.

Anne looked up from a steaming pot of water, her curls drooping and frizzing simultaneously. "There you are. Did you see Uncle Eric?" She leaned forward, whispering to Levi. "I have never seen anyone work so hard and be so happy. He seemed happy to clean the toilets. I hate cleaning the toilets at home."

"Yeah," Levi agreed, tipping the fresh water into Anne's pot, "and ours even flush. Hey, I just learned something…"

SMASH. BANG. CRASH.

A scream sounded from the other side of the kitchen. A rat had jumped from a cupboard onto the head of a kitchen worker, causing her to slip and fall. A stack of clean pots and pans crashed down with her. In the noise and chaos, the rat found a hole and got away before anyone could catch it.

"Peter! Get your trapping team in here!" The woman that served lunch stood with her hands on her hips. "I thought you said you patched all the holes."

Levi helped pick up the pots while others helped the kitchen worker to her feet. The poor woman scratched at her hair and shivered. "I'm going to feel that creature on my head for a week!"

"Where there's a will, there's a way," Anne said, standing on a stool, looking into the hole in the wall. "Looks like the rat chewed a hole to get in."

Peter rubbed his hands together. "I was looking for an opportunity to test out my new trap idea. Annie, would you like to help me?"

"Sure!" Anne said, jumping down from her perch.

Levi wrinkled his nose. "You don't like when I call you Annie."

Anne shushed him. "Peter says it in a British accent."

Levi rolled his eyes and groaned.

CHAPTER 5

Back outside in the cold, Levi and Anne saw a large group of people standing in the middle of what seemed to be a makeshift soccer field. A game had started between a group of teenagers and people had stopped to watch. Almost the entire camp congregated on the dirt to participate in or cheer on the game. The guards sat on the walls and leaned out of the watchtower windows to watch the match.

Levi and Peter were asked to fill in on a few different teams. Anne was confused. "Levi, why are they using a soccer ball if they're going to play football?"

"America is the only place in the world that calls the game soccer. Everywhere else in the world calls it football. So, there's American football and American soccer. Here it's just football," Levi said, tying a scrap of red-colored fabric around his arm to show his team.

"That sort of makes sense. Is Uncle Eric playing?" Anne asked, handing him a cup of water.

"No, he's going to referee the game. I wish he was. I want to see him run. Peter told me Uncle Eric ran the sports program at their school."

Anne nodded her head. "Some of the kitchen ladies were telling me that. I've heard lots of people talking about him and how good of a man he is. He really cares for everyone, and nothing is too much trouble for him. And that Uncle Eric is one of the best runners, so much so that he apparently won an Olympic gold medal."

"Why didn't you tell me that?" Levi squawked indignantly. "It's only the most interesting thing I've ever heard. Why is he in China? Do you think he got captured while running a big race?"

Uncle Eric blew his whistle, effectively halting Levi's torrent of questions.

People huddled together against the cold and cheered and waved for everyone who won and lost. Anne jumped up and down, cheering on Levi and Peter just as loudly as everyone else. No one seemed to be bothered by the two new kids that had just arrived with no warning. Anne spent the game helping the kitchen ladies hand out weak tea in cups and reused tins to those watching the game.

Toward the end of the game, Levi kicked a goal shot and missed, sending the ball wide of the goal. Uncle Eric blew the whistle and took off after the ball. Everyone stopped to watch him sprint across the courtyard after the ball. When he finally caught it, the crowd cheered as if he had scored a goal himself.

Levi stood in the middle of the field, watching a man who could have enjoyed a huge career in the sports world chase a patched ball in a prison yard. He couldn't understand the reason. "Why did you do that, Uncle Eric?" he whispered to himself. "How did you get here? Why did you give up a part of who you are?" Levi's thoughts circled round and round, unable to come up with an explanation for why he and Anne were here. He felt small and lost, like there was a purpose for this, but he couldn't find it.

Uncle Eric was walking up to Levi and his mouth was moving. Levi couldn't hear anything. The world in front of Levi started to blur and change. He turned to look at Anne and her eyes were wide. The wind became stronger, wrapping around them. Anne grabbed his hand, the wind whipping around the two of them as China faded. The world started to spin and tilt, the wind pushing and pulling at their clothes.

Levi yelled, "I'm not ready to go! What's happening now?"

Anne opened her eyes and looked around. They were in an office, surrounded by men in suits, looking very upset. Levi still held her hand and had his eyes closed. "Levi!" Anne whispered, "Open your eyes!"

His eyes snapped open as shock spread over his face. "Oh, I'm so glad we aren't home yet. But where are we now?"

They were in an office with dark wood paneling on the walls and a massive desk at one end of the room. An elderly bald man sat behind the desk, looking over stacks of paper while nervously wiping his forehead with a hand-kerchief. The men were talking in hushed voices while smoking large cigars. The smoke filled the room, making the already hot room feel more depressing and ominous. Even the large Union Jack hanging on the wall seemed to wilt in the heat.

"An office, I think, but I don't know what's going on," Levi said. "I don't think they can see us."

Anne took a step forward and tapped a man wearing a pinstripe suit on his arm. The man brushed his sleeve as if a fly had landed on him. "Cool!" Anne looked at Levi with mischief in her eyes.

"Don't do anything! Look! Is that Uncle Eric?" Levi pointed to the door that opened to reveal a younger Eric dressed in white pants and a blue jacket. He held a straw hat under his arm and smiled while shaking hands with the men in the room.

Anne reached out to try and pull Uncle Eric's hat from his hand. Levi grabbed her hand. "Shh! I want to hear this."

Anne pouted, but put her hand down and paid attention to what the balding older man was saying.

"Now listen, Mr. Liddell, I understand your convictions and I commend you for wanting to stick to them. But this is the United Kingdom's best chance to win a gold medal. It's your duty to your country to win."

Younger Eric smiled. "Sir, I appreciate all you've done for me. Even going so far as to attempt to change the day of the race just for me. However, the fifth commandment says to 'Remember the Sabbath and keep it holy.' In all my years I've kept that commandment, and I do not intend to break it now."

Anne and Levi looked at each other in shock while another man spoke, waving his cigar angrily. "What about your country's honor? This is your chance to make history and a name for yourself as a national hero. Your country is counting on you. You're practically guaranteed a gold medal in the hundred-yard dash."

Eric turned, and in a soft but passionate voice said, "The Lord made me fast, but that's only one part of who I am. The Bible says in 1 Peter 2:17, 'Honour all *men*. Love the brotherhood. Fear God. Honor the king.' You see, sir, honoring the king is second to honoring God. I will not abandon my beliefs for personal or national glory. In fact,

I will be preaching at the Church of Scotland in Paris on that Sunday, if you would like to join us."

The old man choked and wheezed on his cigar, and the rest of the men murmured to each other. "Thank you, my boy, but I have a previous engagement on that day."

Levi whispered, "He's guaranteed to win, and he's just walking away without a second thought. I can't believe it. How could he do that?"

The bald man started speaking again. "Well, Mr. Liddell, if that's your final answer regarding the hundred-yard dash, you do have the opportunity to still run in the 1924 Olympic Games in the four-hundred-meter race. The first heat is on Thursday and the final is on Friday."

Anne whispered, "What does he mean by 'heat?'"

"Because so many athletes want to run in this race, they hold practice races. Only the top two or three go to the final race that wins the medal. Now, shh. I still can't believe what he's doing."

Uncle Eric smiled. "Thank you for your kindness, sir. I will do my best in the four hundred. I am thankful for the opportunity to represent my country in Paris."

"Levi…" Anne saw the world starting to blur as Uncle Eric left the room.

"Surely God won't mind if he runs," Levi mumbled.

"Levi!" The wind started pulling at her hair.

"I mean, even Uncle Eric said that God made him fast."

"LEVI!"

"What?"

"Look!" Anne grabbed his hand as the world spun out of focus once again.

CHAPTER 6

The transport wind seemed to have a habit of dropping them off in extreme temperature differences. The cold took Anne's breath away after being in that hot, stuffy office. The gray skies hanging over the prison camp did not make for a warm welcome back to China. Levi stood like a statue, confused and rattled by what he had just heard.

"Annie!" The voice of Peter cut through the silence of the empty soccer field. Anne turned to see only Peter's legs, for that was all that could be seen under the pile of broken sports equipment and other scraps that waddled toward them.

"Come to Uncle Eric's room. We have some work to do on all this equipment, and Uncle Eric is going to tell us a story."

"Come on, Levi." Anne pulled on Levi's coat, "Maybe he'll tell us the story of his Olympic race. It sounded like he was going to run in at least one race at the Olympics. Plus, Peter already told us he won a gold medal."

Levi shook himself out of his thoughts and followed Anne and the walking junkyard that was Peter into one of the long, barrack-like buildings.

A few other children were already there and helped Peter put down his load. All of them worked to sort out the mess.

A boy pulled a scrap of paper out of the pile, and Peter jumped up to snatch it back and held it behind his back. "Don't look at that! That would be cheating."

"What is it?" asked Anne.

"Come over here," said Peter, sitting down on the floor and leaning up against Uncle Eric's bed. Anne perched on the edge of the bed, looking over Peter's shoulder at the paper. On it was a design for some kind of trap.

Peter said, "Each team must build their own rat trap. Everyone puts out their traps on the same day in different spots. After a set number of days, the team with the biggest rat wins. Sometimes, the only trap with a rat wins. As a prize, the winning team will get something nice for dinner that isn't stew."

Uncle Eric entered the room with a few of the other children. They made themselves comfortable on the beds of Uncle Eric's roommates or found a spot on the floor. Uncle Eric lit the stove and put a used coffee can full of gooey tar on top to heat up. A large pile of broken sports equipment sat in the middle of the common space. Split hockey sticks, balls with holes in them and nets that needed mending were quickly sorted and assigned to teams of children to fix.

Uncle Eric sat down on the floor and pulled a broken net onto his lap. "Alright friends, what would you like to talk about tonight?" Looking at Anne and Levi, he explained, "Every week we have to gather all the equipment to make sure it can be used during the week. While we work, we talk about anything we have questions about. Sometimes we read a book or tell our own stories."

Peter spoke up. "Since Levi and Annie are new, can we hear about you when you were young again?"

Uncle Eric laughed. "What about the rest of you? Would you like to hear that story again?"

"Yes!" The children gathered around, each with a project in their hands, and Uncle Eric began.

"I was born in a place called Siao Chang, which is in northern China, to my parents who were missionaries from Scotland. When I turned six years old, my parents went back to Scotland for a year to rest and visit family. After spending that year with my grandparents in the Highlands, my parents prepared to go back to

China. They decided that my brother and I should stay in Scotland at a boarding school while the rest of the family returned to China."

"Did you miss your parents?" Anne asked while attempting to restitch a hole in a ball.

"I still miss my parents to this day. My father passed away a few years ago. My mother still lives in Scotland, as far as I know. But at the time I had my big brother Robert with me, and I became too busy with school and sports to spend much time missing them.

"I excelled in sports, and between Rob and me, we broke most of the exciting sports records at school. We both played on the school cricket and rugby teams. Rob, being older than me, graduated first and left to enter university. I was extremely shy so he would often talk for me. I did struggle when he left—I had to learn to talk for myself and be more comfortable in group settings.

"Once I graduated from boarding school, I entered the University of Edinburgh to get a science and philosophy degree. I wanted to be a teacher, although I wasn't sure what the Lord had in store for my future. At university, I again joined sports. I was talked into joining the track team as a freshman. They discovered that I'm a very good sprinter, my best event was the one-hundred-meter. I managed to break all the records that were previously set in the school.

"I was also on the school's rugby team where I played as a wing. My job was to get the ball as close to the other team's goal line as possible. In my sophomore year, we won six of seven games. Because of this, I was invited to play on Scotland's national Ruby team. Scotland's biggest rival is Wales, and we hadn't won a game since 1890. We beat Wales with a score of eleven to eight."

The boys broke out in cheers and ran around the room waving hockey sticks and chanting, "UNCLE ERIC! UNCLE ERIC! The Greatest Sportsman Ever!" A wrestling match started that ended with a bucket of water spilling and Anne having to catch the can of tar before it spilled as well.

Peter yelled, "I wish I could have seen that game! Down with Wales!"

Uncle Eric winced and placed his hand on his forehead, closing his eyes for a moment. "Settle down lads, or we'll never get this job done." The noise quieted, and he reopened his eyes with a smile. The boys settled back down and reorganized the equipment.

Anne passed a ball with a hole in it to Levi, who was watching the tar pot slowly bubble on the stove. Levi carefully used a stick to spread the tar to plug the hole. Anne whispered to him, "Do you hear how humbly he talks about himself? One of the kitchen ladies told me he's never lost more than two races."

Levi blew on the tar. "I know. I really hope he'll tell his Olympic story. He's really inspiring. I just wish I could understand why he didn't continue running. He obviously excels at it. Why did he quit? Especially in the Olympics, the whole country was expecting him to run if he was that famous."

Anne nodded, carefully poking the tar to see if it had cooled yet. "I've heard some people find him annoying. The most common complaint I've heard is he won't do anything on Sundays. It's the Lord's day. He helps lead a church service every week."

Levi put the tar back on the stove. "I wonder if he's always been like that. We always go to church, I didn't know there was more. According to what he said in the office, he really means that. It cost him an almost guaranteed gold medal. Which is *crazy*."

With all the sports equipment fixed and put away, it was time for supper. Back in the dining hall with the rest of the camp, they had tinned meat with vegetable soup and a chocolate cookie. The meat and chocolate had come in the Red Cross packages that morning.

Peter took a bite, closed his eyes, and sighed. "Ah, I love when the Red Cross arrives. The food is always better. For a few days at least."

Anne wasn't paying attention to her food. Instead, she was staring in horror at the monstrous cockroach crawling up Levi's back.

Levi turned to see what Anne was looking at, accidentally bringing the object of Anne's fear closer to her.

"EKKK! Get away from me!" Anne shrieked.

"Hold still, laddie." Uncle Eric appeared and calmly wiped the offending bug off Levi's sweater, crushing it under his foot. A satisfying crunch caused Anne to shudder and pull her jacket closer. "I hate bugs. Ugh!"

Levi smirked and Peter laughed, saying, "You get used to the bugs after a while. Good source of protein, but no one can seem to get past the putrid taste."

Levi looked impressed. "I've had crickets. And in the summer, I love finding cicada skins left behind on trees. Tastes like saltless potato chips."

Anne gagged, and Peter laughed.

Levi turned to Anne. "You're terrified of bugs, yet you're sticking your nose in a rat hole. You're an enigma for sure."

Anne shrugged. "Rats are cute."

Later that night, Anne lay in her bed in the children's dorm and listened to the rat crawling around in the rafters. "I will catch you, you dirty rat."

A shower of dust rained down on her as if the rat was taunting her by saying, "I'd like to see you try."

CHAPTER 7

The next morning, as Levi broke the ice on the water bucket to wash his face, a thought struck him, and he froze. He rushed to get dressed and found Anne in the breakfast line.

"Anne!" he whispered, pulling her out of line. "How are we going to get home? What if we're stuck here forever?"

Anne's eyes widened, and she said, "I don't know! I didn't think about it until just now."

Levi rubbed his face and pulled on his collar. "I guess we should just wait and see what happens. We can clearly time travel. I'm just not sure how to get home. Maybe another portal will open and that's how we get home."

"Let's stick together as much as we can so we don't miss it," Anne said, stepping back in line. "I heard we're having eggs for breakfast this morning. I don't know where they came from. I haven't seen any chickens in the compound."

The same lunch lady from yesterday handed each of them a thick piece of bread that had been sliced open and scrambled eggs stuffed inside.

Levi took the sandwich with a thank you and mumbled to Anne, "Maybe it's a 'don't ask, don't tell' sort of thing? I saw one of the monks walking by this morning hiding something under his robe." They took a seat at one of the large tables.

Peter arrived, sitting down next to Levi with a bowl of porridge instead of a sandwich. "Good morning!" He gulped down his porridge in large spoonfuls, talking with his mouth full. "Today is Friday, so we only have a half day of classes. The rest of the day is for sporting matches. Uncle Eric organizes different races and games to keep us entertained."

A horn sounded loudly and Peter grabbed his dishes. "Come on! If we hurry, we can catch Uncle Eric and ask him about the games he has planned today."

Pulling on their coats and hats, the three children ran out of the dining hall and raced to Uncle Eric's room. A sign that read, "Eric is In" hung on the door.

A very strange sight met their eyes when they pushed open the door. Three men were chasing a wildly crowing rooster around the small bedroom. When the rooster saw the half-open door, he made a run for it.

Anne slammed the door shut while Levi and Peter dropped to the floor to each catch a leg of the frantic chicken. The poor creature started crowing even louder until one of the men quickly dropped a blanket over its eyes and it instantly stopped yelling.

Everyone breathed a sigh, but stayed quiet. Uncle Eric slowly looked out a slit in the paper-covered window. "I don't see anyone," he whispered.

"Where did this come from?" Anne asked, still leaning on the door.

The man with the blanket carefully picked up the chicken, keeping its eyes covered. "Someone saw it on the roof of the toilets this morning, caught it and brought it in here. Eric, you should take the children to the schoolhouse. The guards get suspicious when you aren't on time. We don't need them coming in here. We'll take care of the chicken."

"Good thinking. Come children, let's go." Uncle Eric hurried out the door, pulling on his coat.

Anne fell in step next to Uncle Eric. "We're going to eat that chicken for lunch, aren't we?"

Uncle Eric chuckled and put his arm around Anne's shoulders. "Yes lass, it isn't a laying chicken, and it would only get us into trouble with the guards if we let it loose."

Anne sighed and changed the subject. "Peter says today is a half day. Does this mean we get to hear the rest of your story?"

Uncle Eric laughed. "Well, since I haven't had a chance to see what level of school you two have had, I suppose that can wait till Monday."

"WOOHOO!" Peter and Levi jumped in the air and took off, sprinting toward the schoolroom. By the time Anne arrived with Uncle Eric, the fire was lit in the stove and the children were ready and eager to listen.

"Alright, well, I had been praying for many years about what to do after I graduated from the University of Edinburgh. All of my family were still missionaries in China, so I joined them in June of 1925. I applied and was granted a job at the Tientsin Anglo-Chinese College. It's an all-boys Christian school, mostly for the children of missionaries and businessmen that lived in and around Tientsin. I was hired as a science teacher, but soon became the athletic director as well. I went back to Scotland for a year to train to become a minister in 1932. When I returned to Tientsin, I was given more responsibilities at the school. I also began speaking at churches and other meetings in the city and surrounding areas."

"Uncle Eric!" Peter interrupted. "Tell us how you got the nickname 'The Flying Scotsman.'"

Uncle Eric grimaced and rubbed at his hip. "That is a painful memory, my boy. Well, I enjoyed running and was still relatively well-known in the racing world. I had been asked to run in a race in the very north of China as part of the opening ceremonies of the new sports stadium I helped design. I had just thirty minutes to run the race before my boat was supposed to leave to take me back home to Tientsin. So, I ran the race, jumped in a taxi, and raced down to the dock. The boat had already started pulling away from the dock by the time I got there. So, I decided to run down the dock at full speed to see if I could jump onto the deck of the boat. The boat was still moving slowly. I threw my suitcase first and some of the passengers on the boat caught it for me. By the grace of God, a wave pushed the boat back towards the dock just as I jumped off the end of the dock into the air. I just cleared the railing and landed safely, albeit a little bruised on the boat. I think someone took a picture of the jump. I've never seen it. I did read in the paper afterward that the bystanders think I jumped about fifteen feet."

Levi raised his hand. "Uncle Eric, didn't you run in the Olympics? Why haven't you talked about that? I don't understand why you gave up a career running when you're clearly good at it to be in China in a prison camp, of all places."

Anne looked scandalized by the way Levi blurted out question after question. *He's really confused about this,* she thought. *I wonder why he's so anxious to understand.*

Uncle Eric paused and his face turned thoughtful. "You know, laddie, the boys in my Bible study at school asked me the same questions. They wanted to know why someone like me who could have gotten so much 'worldly honor' would give it all up to come to China. I have always seen my ability to run as a gift. The Lord made me for a purpose. He made me for China. But he also made me fast. And when I run, I feel his pleasure. For me to win, honors Him. But I count it as a greater purpose to serve His people than to serve myself by winning."

Anne watched a change fall over Levi. She could tell his mind was racing and his mood had changed. He sank into himself, trying to understand how the Lord could give such a unique gift, only to ask Uncle Eric to give it up.

A horn sounded through the quiet of the schoolroom. "Well"—Uncle Eric stood—"it looks like it's time for lunch, and afterwards we're off to the races!"

The room came alive with chatter, but Levi stayed seated, lost in thought.

When there was no one left in the room, Anne pulled at Levi's sleeve. "Come on. A game and some exercise will do you good.

CHAPTER 8

Anne and Levi pulled on their coats and stepped through the door. A gust of wind slammed into them, pushing them back through the door and into another whirlwind of wind and colors.

"What's happening now?" Levi yelled over the wind. "This is getting old."

The wind stopped, only to be replaced by the roaring of a crowd. Levi and Anne opened their eyes to find themselves in an open-air stadium filled with thousands of people. *Colombes Stadium, Paris, France* was spelled out around the top of the overhang that provided the only shade. Flags from forty-five different countries hung limp in the still, hot air. A rugby field sat in the center of the stadium with a black cinder track surrounding it. Two seating areas for fans faced each other from opposite sides of the field. The sun was slowly setting, casting long shadows over the field. A huge white flag with the Olympic rings hung in the place of honor at the top of the stadium.

"Annie!" Levi exclaimed. "We're at the Olympics!"

Anne gasped at the sight of women in great big hats and long dresses with strings of pearls and heavy earrings. She looked down and was pleased to see she was wearing a knee-length, short-sleeved, bright-pink dress with small black shoes. Instead of a hat, which disappointed her greatly, she found that she was holding a lacy light-pink parasol, which she promptly opened and settled over her shoulder. "Finally, I get to wear something I like."

Levi asked a gentleman standing nearby for a newspaper. Splashed across the top of the paper was, *ERIC LIDDELL THE MAN WHO WOULDN'T RUN ON A SUNDAY.* The article went on to say that Eric Liddell was a traitor to his country by not competing in the event for which he was the favorite to win. Instead, he was going to run in a race that was four times his usual distance. It also stated that on Sunday, Eric Liddell was preaching in a local church instead of honoring his country.

"Anne, look at this." Levi turned to show her the newspaper and noticed her holding her parasol. "Why do you have an umbrella? It's not raining."

Anne put her hand on her hip and brandished the thing in question, nearly taking the hat off a gentleman behind her. "Oops, excuse me. I'm sorry." She put her arm down rather sheepishly and returned her attention to Levi. "I guess we aren't invisible here. This"—pointing over her shoulder—"is a parasol. It's made to keep the sun off a lady's face and neck when a hat is inappropriate. It has been made out of the prettiest lace I've ever seen and I should very much like to take it home with me. Now that you have been corrected in your terminology, what were you trying to tell me?"

Completely unfazed by her ramblings, Levi chuckled and handed her the paper, and pointed to the headline. As she read it, he looked around. He glanced down at his new outfit, a pair of shorts with a button shirt and a jacket that he quickly took off as he noticed the heat of the day.

Anne rattled the paper in indignation at what it said about Uncle Eric. "How can they say that about him? They don't even know him! He's the best, most kind man I have ever met!"

"Anne, calm down!" Levi picked up a race program and looked at the big clock attached to the column above Anne's head. "According to this, I think the race Uncle Eric is going to be in is about to start. I want to see him run. I don't know how close to the rail we can get. Let's find a good seat to see him."

A man walking by stopped when he heard Levi's question. He wore a blue suit and a straw hat. A pin on his jacket said, *Great Britain Coach Staff.* He came over and asked, "Are you two children fans of Eric Liddell?"

Anne answered, "I'm not a child. I'm twelve years old."

Levi shushed her and said, "Yes sir. We're here to see him run. I'm Levi and this is Anne."

The man smiled. "Pleased to meet you both. I'm also here to see him run. But we won't be able to see anything from here. Come with me. I have seats by the starting line, but you can see the finish line from the seats."

"Sir, I don't mean to be rude, but who are you?" Anne asked.

"Good question, young lady. I'm Tom McKerchar, a friend of Eric's. I've known him for a long, long time. He doesn't know I'm here. All of his family are in China and aren't able to come to support him. I've seen him run many times. But I know that this time will be very special."

They followed Mr. McKerchar down the stairs of the stadium, to the front row where the starting line was positioned. Mr. McKerchar handed Levi a program that had all the runners' names and running numbers listed by country. Levi was occupied with matching the runners milling around on the track in front of them with the countries they represented. Without taking his eyes off the track, Levi asked, "The hundred-meter dash is his best event, right?"

Mr. McKerchar nodded. "I've never seen him run more than two hundred meters. I have no doubt that he'll do his best, but I don't know how he'll be able to pull off a win running four times his usual distance. He also drew the outside lane, which is the hardest to run in. He'll start slightly ahead of the rest of the pack but will most likely lose that advantage as the race goes on. You also can't see if someone is closing behind you."

Mr. McKerchar signaled a passing vendor selling cold lemonade. Quickly picking up two, he handed one to Anne who was grateful for the cooling refreshment and said thank you. The other he gave to Levi before handing the man a few coins. Anne sipped on her drink, thankful for the shade of her parasol. Levi didn't seem to feel the heat, scanning the track for a glimpse of Uncle Eric.

Bagpipes began playing and the crowd cheered as Uncle Eric walked out onto the track. Levi thought he heard a few people boo as well. Wearing white shorts and a white t-shirt with the number 451 pinned to the front of his shirt, he smiled and waved to the crowd. Levi and Anne cheered and waved with the rest of the crowd.

He shook hands with the five other racers before prepping his lane for the race. Taking a small trowel, he dug two small holes for his toes to rest in when he assumed his starting position. When the bagpipes finished their song and Eric saluted them, the crowd fell silent. The stadium crackled with suspense.

The racers crouched in their lanes, waiting for the starting gun.

Everyone collectively held their breath, waiting to see what would unfold right in front of their eyes.

CRACK!

The starting gun fired, and the runners exploded from the line.

Eric was the first in front. He sprinted toward the first turn, his legs pumping. Horatio Fitch, a well-known American runner, was the favorite to win the race, pacing himself slightly behind. As they made the first turn, which was the halfway point, Levi and Anne stood and leaned over the railing, craning their necks to see.

With 200 meters down, Eric was still in front. Levi's knuckles turned white, he was holding the railing so tight. He knew that Eric shouldn't have sprinted to start the race. He wouldn't have enough speed to finish.

Eric's arms spun wildly, making him look like a windmill. His chest puffed out with his face toward the sky.

Horatio edged up on Eric, waiting for him to exhaust himself. Levi held his breath, willing Eric to go faster. Eric seemed to hear Levi's silent plea and his arms went faster and so did his feet.

100 meters to go, the crowd was on their feet. Horatio trailed Eric, working to catch up to him but steadily falling behind. The rest of the runners spread out along the track.

Eric's head flew back farther to look at the sky and his arms pumped in rhythm to his pounding legs. It seemed that he was running faster than when he started. The track behind him looked like it was smoking from the puffs of cinder kicked up by his feet. Levi stood up straight, clinging to the railing. "*Don't fall, don't fall Uncle Eric, this is it!*" he silently chanted, unable to make his voice work. Horatio was still in second but was falling farther behind, unable to catch him. The rest of the field was trailing miserably.

The crowd roared and rose to its feet as Eric made the final turn. They cheered and encouraged Eric almost as if they had forgotten they doubted him just minutes before.

Eric flew across the finish line and kept running. He only started to slow when he saw the finish line banner over his head. The finish line tape snapped across his chest, confirming his win. Eric Liddell had won the 400-meter race, six meters ahead of Horatio Finch.

Anne and Levi screamed and jumped up and down. Strangers were hugging each other and cheering Eric's name.

Levi looked at Mr. McKerchar who was holding a stopwatch, staring at it in disbelief. He showed it to Levi. The time showed 47.6 seconds. With tears in his eyes, he said to Levi, "He just broke the world record."

Levi stared out, watching Eric being carried around the track on the shoulders of his teammates while the band played Great Britain's national anthem, "God Save the King." The parade stopped in front of the British Royal Box. The prince stood and applauded, nodding his head in respect to Britain's newest hero.

The noise from the crowd began to fade. The now familiar wind started pulling on Levi's shirt. He looked at Anne, who had tears streaming down her face. She leaned in and Levi wrapped his arms around her as they shut their eyes for the ride.

CHAPTER 9

A voice popped the quiet bubble that surrounded Levi and Anne. "Anne!"

It was cold again, a sharp change from the sweltering stadium. Anne opened her eyes and saw that Paris was gone and they were back in the prison camp.

"The kitchen ladies saw the rat again! Hurry, let's set up our trap!" The voice belonged to Peter, who stood across the field, waving.

"Drat, I didn't hold on to that parasol." She looked up at Levi, who was lost in thought. She pulled on his jacket and asked, "Are you ok?"

Levi looked around and said, "I have questions. It was the biggest race of his life and he could have become a superstar athlete. He just gave it all up." He pulled on his cap in frustration.

Anne waved at Peter. "Why don't you find Uncle Eric and ask him about it? I'm sure he'll be willing to talk to you. I'm going to go with Peter to catch that rat that's plaguing the kitchen."

She took off across the field as Levi turned and walked toward the men's dormitories, his mind spinning with questions.

He found Uncle Eric in his room, laying on his bed with his eyes closed. When the door opened, Eric sat up and motioned Levi to come in.

"What can I do for you, my boy?" he said with a smile, holding a hand to his head and closing his eyes for a moment.

"Are you alright?"

"Oh yes, laddie. I get headaches from time to time so I have to take a rest, but I'm just dandy now. How can I help you?"

"I have questions, sir. Why did you give up a gold medal to go to church? That just seems like the craziest thing to me. Surely since God made you fast, He would forgive you for running on Sunday."

Uncle Eric smiled and motioned Levi to sit down on an old trunk next to his bed. "It seems like you've heard my story. I'm very glad you did. During that time, a lot of people tried to justify that The Lord would permit me to break my beliefs for one time, especially for such an important event.

"But." Levi started.

"Hold on laddie. I'll explain. I was taught my whole life that Sunday is the day that we focus on the Lord, and nothing is more important than that. For me to break that personal conviction would be, in my eyes, a sin. Not everyone has the same conviction as I do, and that's between them and the Lord. It's not for me to judge. While a lot of people thought and said cruel things about me and my decision, I knew the Lord would honor my sacrifice. In the end, it didn't matter to me if I won a medal or not because I run for the Lord and not for my own gain. My only job was to run as fast as I could and leave the result in His hands."

Levi sat with his thoughts spinning. "Well, you did break a world record for a race that you never trained for, so I suppose that would be God honoring your sacrifice."

Eric nodded. "On that Sunday, when I was supposed to be running in the hundred-meter, I preached a sermon on Isaiah 40:28-31. It says, 'Have you not known? Have you not heard? The everlasting God, the LORD, The Creator of the ends of the earth, neither faints nor is weary. His understanding is unsearchable. He gives power to the weak, and to those who have no might, He increases strength. Even the youths shall faint and be weary, and the young men shall utterly fall, but those who wait on the LORD Shall renew their strength; They shall mount up with wings like eagles, They shall run and not be weary, They shall walk and not faint.'"

Uncle Eric opened his eyes and smiled. "You see, laddie, even if I had lost the race, it still would have been an honor for the Lord. He gave me the strength to finish so I could proclaim that the Lord is mighty and honors those who serve him."

Levi took a deep breath. "I have a kid on my baseball team that no one likes to have around. His name is Charlie, he wants to be a part of the team, but he can't hit or catch a ball to save his life. So, Coach made him the water boy. He's very loud and difficult to be friends with. He's in my Sunday school class and he always says that we're friends. The guys on the team don't like him and if I become friends with Charlie, they may ignore me and not want to be friends anymore."

Uncle Eric nodded his head and thought for a minute before answering. "I can understand why this is a difficult choice. I do know what it feels like to be convicted to do something hard that other people may not understand. I can't tell you what to do. It's important that you search your heart and think about what you would do if Charlie was Jesus."

"Well, if I thought Charlie was Jesus, I would obviously want to be friends with him no matter what anyone else thought of me."

Uncle Eric reached under his pillow and pulled out a well-worn Bible. "It's easy to say that in theory. It's much more difficult to walk that out in practice."

He opened the Bible and read, "in Matthew 25 during the final judgment of all people the Lord will say to the righteous, 'For I was hungry and you gave me food, I was thirsty and you gave me drink, I was a stranger and you welcomed me, I was naked and you clothed me, I was sick and you visited me, I was in prison and you came to me.' And the righteous will ask when did they see the Lord this way? The Lord will respond, 'Whatever you do for the least of these you do for me.'"

Gently closing the book, Uncle Eric leaned on his knees. "Taking the time to be friends with Charlie might turn the team against you, or you could be the one to change their view about Charlie. Either way, you will be an example of how to treat others who are different. It's a hard choice, but I know you will make a good decision."

Levi hung his head. "I feel like I've really messed up."

Uncle Eric put his hand on his shoulder, and Levi looked up into his clear blue eyes. "There's still time. The Lord doesn't hold our mistakes against us. We always have His forgiveness before we even ask for it. That's the beauty of being a Christian. As a Christian, Levi, I challenge you. Have great aim—have a high standard—make Jesus your ideal. Make Him an ideal not merely to be admired, but also to be followed."

Levi sat up straight and nodded with tears in his eyes. "Thank you, Uncle Eric. I know what I have to do."

Uncle Eric shook Levi's hand and, with tears in his own eyes, said, "I'm very proud of you, son. You'll do the right thing. Rely on the Lord for your strength because it will be hard."

"Yes, sir."

Uncle Eric flipped open his Bible again and started writing on a blank page.

Levi thought to himself that this conversation was the reason for the trip to China and for meeting Uncle Eric. Not only did he get to spend a few days with an Olympic champion who had an amazing victory story, but the same man also spoke exactly what Levi needed to hear.

Even if this is just a dream, Levi thought, *God had made it clear what He wants me to do.*

CHAPTER 10

Without ceremony, the door to Uncle Eric's room flew open with a bang. Levi, still lost in thought, jumped and nearly slipped off the rounded top of the trunk, and Uncle Eric looked up calmly from the scrap of paper he was writing on.

Peter and Anne appeared panting for air, and at the sight of Levi's face started laughing. "Works every time!" Anne gasped. Uncle Eric chuckled and slipped the paper into Levi's jacket, which was sitting on the bed, without Levi noticing.

Levi folded his arms and sulked while Peter held up what was in his hands. A large can had been nailed to a piece of scrap wood and awful sounds were coming from it.

Anne proudly proclaimed, "It's a rat trap! We put a tiny bit of bait at the center of the cuts and laid the whole thing on its side. When the rat went for the food, he pushed through into the can. His weight then tipped it upright so he can't get out."

Uncle Eric came over for a closer look. The top of the can was carefully cut like a pie, and the points of the pie were slightly bent inward, where the rat had pushed through the cuts.

"And," Peter added, "because the points are so sharp and bent inward, it can't push its way out."

"That is ingenious! I'm very impressed," Uncle Eric praised while Levi backed up a step. The rat let out an angry hiss as Peter shook the trap.

"We were the only team that caught something this time. No one wants to open the trap to measure how big it is." Peter laughed and added, "Unless Levi wants to volunteer his services. The guards are going to give us a can of beans as a prize, and the kitchen ladies will give us a piece of chocolate with lunch."

"Why am I friends with you? Two peas in a pod, both of you," Levi grumbled, looking with disgust at the hissing and scratching can.

"Beans on toast for me!" Peter sang on his way out the door.

Anne laughed while Peter took the hissing, rattling can outside.

Anne came over and hugged Levi. "Did you talk to him?"

Levi smiled and nodded. "Yeah, I did. I know why he chose the way he did. He also helped me see what to do about Charlie. I'm ready to go home now."

Anne said, "I don't want to leave. I love Uncle Eric, and what's going to happen to these people?" She had already started to cry.

"We can't stay here forever, though."

Uncle Eric walked over and gave each of them a hug. "It was a pleasure to meet both of you. Don't worry about us, the Lord will provide. We all have our race to run, and I'm close to the end of my race."

Laying a hand on each of them, he prayed, "Father, protect Anne and Levi and show them your love and strength to make the difficult choices in front of them. Thank you for your Son who bore all our sins and the freedom we live in because of Him. We bless you, Lord. Amen."

He smiled and wiped the tears from Anne's eyes and shook Levi's hand. A horn sounded, and Uncle Eric pulled on his coat. Peter stuck his head through the door and waved before Uncle Eric walked out the door.

Anne pointed at the doorframe; it had started to glow. This time, a gentle wind pushed at their backs, guiding them to the door.

Levi nodded, and holding hands, the two of them walked through the door. Flashes of color danced in front of their eyes until all noise stopped.

They were standing in the attic, back in their normal clothes. The rain had stopped. Sun poured in the window, lighting up the still-open chest. The book sat abandoned on the floor, looking normal and not magical at all. On the cover, Uncle Eric was frozen in time at the finish line.

Anne said, "I'm a little scared to touch it."

Levi picked it up.

"I wonder what happened to Uncle Eric," Anne continued, picking up the purple hat off the floor.

Levi opened the book to the last chapter and read aloud.

During Eric Liddell's imprisonment in the Weihsien Internment Camp, he was a light to every person in the camp, especially among the youth. There was a rumor that the British government attempted to conduct a prisoner swap with Japan for Eric's freedom. It was said that he gave his release to a pregnant woman. On February 21, 1945, Eric Liddell passed away from an undiagnosed brain tumor while still imprisoned. He was not only a well-known Olympic athlete and a kind and generous soul, but a man who loved the Lord and ran his race well. On a scrap of paper found among Eric's belongings written on the day he died, he wrote, "All will be well."

Later that summer, on August 16, 1945, eleven days after the Allies bombed Hiroshima, Japan, an American B-24 Liberator bomber named "Armored Angel" swooped low overhead the camp and opened its belly to release U.S. Army paratroopers. The guards of Weihsien did not try to stop the internees from rushing out of the gates to welcome their liberators falling from the sky.

Not a shot was fired during the liberation of the camp. Other planes followed the first, dropping food and supplies till the transport planes arrived.

When the world learned that Eric Liddell had died, memorial services were held in his honor all around the world. Two funds were started in his name. One was to help care for his wife Florence and his three daughters who remained in Canada. The second was the Eric Liddell Challenge Trophy, to be awarded for the best performance at the Scottish Schools Athletic Association track meets. In later years, many books would be written about his remarkable life, and even a film, *Chariots of Fire*, which won the Academy Award for Best Picture in 1981.

Levi closed the book and placed it carefully in the chest. "We must have met him a few months before he died. When I went to speak to him, he was laying down on his bed with his eyes closed. He tried not to show how much pain he was in when he sat up."

Anne wiped her eyes for the second time that day. "I'm not sure how we were able to meet him, but I'll never forget him. It's so sad that he wasn't able to be released."

"Uncle Eric wouldn't say that. He would say he ran his race well, and that's all that matters."

"Kids! Are you still up there?" Auntie M's voice floated up the stairs, popping the solemn mood. "Levi! Your coach just called—your game starts in thirty minutes. Hurry up and come down."

"Coming Mom!" Levi closed the lid on the chest and slipped the key into his pocket. Looking at Anne, he pulled a curl and said, "He was released. He went home with Jesus. Uncle Eric wouldn't want us to be sad. He would want us to keep running our race. So come on, let's go. I have something I need to do."

CHAPTER 11

The car pulled to a stop near the baseball field. Levi grabbed his gear out of the back of the car and headed for the dugout. "Chester Wolf Pack," painted in faded colors, stretched across the cinderblock wall. A long, well-worn bench occupied the back wall. Names and indicators of past players had been carved into the wood and filled in with years of dirt, dust and pine tar. Above the bench, at regular intervals, cheap plastic milk crates hung from makeshift lockers and storage. A chain-link fence closed off the space, the top bent and crooked from years of players and coaches leaning on it.

His coach clapped him on the shoulder. "Hurry and warm up, kid, we don't have much time."

"Sure thing, Coach." Levi emptied his pockets and found the key to the chest in the attic. He put it carefully in a pocket in his bag, not seeing the small piece of paper stuck to the handle. Levi stopped to grab a water bottle off Charlie's table.

Charlie stood proudly in his special spot right by the stairs so he could easily hand water to the players coming and going off the field. He wore a homemade team jersey, a plain blue t-shirt with "Wolf Pack" written badly across the front, and "Water Boy" on the back in white marker.

The field was slightly soggy, and the air was still and muggy. The sun went down, painting the sky in a rainbow of colors. As the lights came on over the field, family and friends cheered and clapped from the metal bleachers and rickety beach chairs. Charlie kept all the water bottles filled and ready to go. He clapped and cheered constantly. Sometimes for the wrong team by accident. This earned him some eye rolls from some of the team, but the rest of the team mostly ignored him. Levi watched with new eyes and felt ashamed of how his team was treating Charlie.

This changes tonight, he thought to himself. *We also need to get him a proper jersey.*

The game started slow for both teams. It was still early in the season, but as the ninth inning came, the Wolf Pack was up by one.

Levi was up to bat and centered his feet. The pitcher wound up and released the ball, and time slowed. He tracked the ball like a heat-seeking missile... *whap*. The ball sank into the catcher's mitt.

"Strike one!" the umpire boomed.

Levi put the bat down and shook out his arms. He looked over his shoulder at his team and then out on the field to his teammate and best friend, Zachary Stevens, crouched on second base.

He took a deep breath and felt his heart rate slow. The ball left the pitcher's hand and Levi swung, clipping the ball and sending it out of bounds.

"Strike two!"

"Come on, Levi!"

"Focus, man!"

"You can do it!"

Proud parents in lawn chairs whistled and held onto their tumblers, watching the game intently. Younger siblings rattled the batting cage, cheering and offering tidbits and tips from their tee-ball games.

Levi smacked the plate with the bat and reset his feet. Blocking out all the cheering and advice, he narrowed his eyes and relaxed his body. The pitcher's arm swung, and the red stitches on the baseball came closer and closer.

POP!

The bat made full contact and the ball hit reverse, sailing high back over the pitcher's mound and into the outfield.

Levi's heart rate matched his pounding feet as he rounded the bases, checking that Stevens had made it home. The crowd was on its feet, screaming and cheering. He rounded third base, looking just in time to see an outfielder running to catch the ball.

Kicking into high gear, Levi sprinted for home, remembering Uncle Eric running to win the gold medal in Paris all those years ago.

Anne watched the ball fly from player to player, making its way to home plate. Levi came closer and closer, Coach motioning wildly for a slide as the ball sailed overhead. A spray of mud hid the last moments from the crowd's view.

"Safe!"

The crowd erupted with cheers. Levi was hoisted on the shoulders of his team, his face streaked with mud and a big smile on his face. *Just like Uncle Eric,* he thought.

After the coach gave his post-game speech, he informed the team of the plan for ice cream at the Spotted Cow in town.

Levi was putting his gear in his bag when he noticed a small piece of paper on the bottom. Picking it up, he read, "Run for something bigger than gold, Run for Him. All will be well. - Eric Liddell."

"Hey Conlon. You coming for ice cream?" Stevens asked.

Looking down at the paper again, Levi answered, "Yeah I am, but Charlie is coming too."

"Huh?"

"I won't go unless Charlie comes too. He's a part of this team."

Stevens stared at Levi like he'd grown three heads. "Ok, I guess."

Levi hurried to catch Charlie, who was collecting the water bottles. "Hey Charlie! Ask your dad if you can come to ice cream with us. My mom can drop you off if you need it."

Charlie's face lit up. "Really? I can come?" He dropped the water bottles in the bucket and bounced up and down like a pinball.

Levi laughed. "Sure you can come. You're a part of the team."

He didn't miss the strange looks his team was throwing his way as they got into the cars. On the way to the ice cream shop, he silently prayed that his team wouldn't shut him out for including Charlie.

When Levi arrived at the Spotted Cow, he was shocked to see that the whole team had gathered around Charlie as he drew on a napkin his predictions for the major league baseball season.

"LEVI!" Charlie's eyes lit up at the sight of his hero and he waved excitedly from across the small ice cream parlor.

Stevens jogged over, keeping an eye on the four-scoop cone clutched in his hand. "Don't get me wrong, Conlon, he's still annoying. But he really knows his baseball."

Joey Lockmore, the shortstop, joined the conversation as Levi ordered his ice cream. "Maybe Coach can get him to analyze the teams we play for the rest of the season."

Levi smiled to himself as his teammates debated on how best to incorporate Charlie's newfound skills into the team. He reached into his pocket and touched the small piece of paper that Uncle Eric had given him.

All was well indeed.

Acknowledgments

To my Heavenly Father, Jesus, and the Holy Spirit for the idea and strength to complete this vision.

To my parents for their unwavering support and strength. Especially to my mom for diligently and successfully homeschooling me so I can be the best version of myself and pursue my dreams.

To my sister and brother-in-law, the best built-in best friends anyone could ask for. This book is for my future nieces and nephews.

To the rest of my family and friends who have been with me for all the ups and downs. I am blessed beyond measure to have such support around me at all times.

To my coach, Barbara Hartzler and my editor Shavonne Clarke from Motif Edits, thank you for your patience with my endless emails and questions. You have contributed greatly to the polish of this adventure.

Further Reading

Eric Liddell Something Greater than Gold - Janet and Geoff Benge

Shantung Compound The story of men and women under pressure - Langdon Gilkey

For The Glory Eric Liddell's Journey From Olympic Champion to Modern Martyr - Duncan Hamilton

The Flying Scotsman A Biography - Sally Magnusson

A Boy's War - David Michell

Chariots of Fire, 1981, Rated PG

Contact me

If you enjoyed this book or are looking for updates on upcoming Levi and Anne adventures sign up for the Kingdom Chasers newsletter @ kingdomchaserspubl.com

Follow @kingdom_charsers_publ on Instagram for writing content and even more updates.

Please feel free to leave a review on Amazon, it would be greatly appreciated.

Author Bio

Reid Billing grew up in a small town in rural New Jersey with her nose in a book. Her love of literature sparked a desire to write from an early age, but it wasn't until she completed her degree in nursing that she was able to write her first manuscript. Currently employed as a postpartum nurse, she makes time to pursue her passion for writing. Her hope is that through these engaging stories, future generations will be inspired to stand by their convictions and love Jesus with all their hearts. Acts 1:8

Made in the USA
Las Vegas, NV
08 June 2024

90899091R00059